Finding Inner Freedom

Mark Anthony Hoffman

Copyright © 2020 Mark Anthony Hoffman.

All Rights Reserved. This book contains material protected under International and Federal Copyright Laws and Treaties. Any unauthorized reprint or use of this material is prohibited. No part of this book may be reproduced or transmitted in any form or by any means, electronic or mechanical, including photocopying, recording, or by any information storage and retrieval system without express written permission from the author/publisher.

Paperback: 978-1-64184-291-4
Ebook: 978-1-64184-292-1

markanthonyhoffman@protonmail.com.

Dedicated to my father, Anthony Hoffman, who taught me, from an early age, the value of inquisitiveness.

Failure dissolves the ego until all that remains is essence.

PREFACE

This book synthesizes a lifetime of exploration, contemplation, and study. The contents represent my understanding of reality and our place in it based on my own insights, wedded with wisdom shared by many others through their teachings and writings. Much of what is stated here is strictly subjective. Many of the assertions presented cannot be proven or otherwise substantiated.

Since my early years I have had a deep interest in science. In college, I found my favorite course to be physics. I was fascinated by exploration of the fundamental processes and principles in the physical universe.

Subsequently, I discovered philosophy, and one might say, I fell in love for the first time. Later, I discovered metaphysics. To deeply contemplate life and man's role was an irresistible magnet, for it allowed me to apply the mental discipline learned through my engineering curriculum to study of the mental, emotional, and spiritual sides of life. This exploration has continued for my entire adult life. For a period of almost twenty years, I read books only on spirituality, religion, mysticism, etc., while concurrently nursing an ever-growing inclination for deep meditation.

Some might call me a "scientist-philosopher." I always looked for a tangible perspective on the spiritual insights I encountered. I found the writings of Indian mystics too obtuse to be fully understood by anyone not already having their inner experience. Part of the challenge they, and any spiritual writer, face is that the necessary words do not exist in language until enough of the population perceives a need for such words.

One goal in this book is to provide a practical, tangible understanding of insights and principles. Another goal is to integrate my science and philosophical studies, along with my personal insights, into a cogent paradigm. My wish is that the content of this book not be construed as dogma—the world has enough of that—but instead, its concepts and ideas be contemplated. It is my hope that the ideas and principles presented here can benefit others on the path.

Mark Anthony Hoffman

1

In the Beginning, God made Man

This book began when I was born. Why do I say that? Because the influences and experiences that molded me began at that instant. Actually, some influences began while I was still in the womb, but since I was not yet "officially" in my body prior to birth, I will simply state that this all started at birth.

At that moment, my awareness in this existence began to grow, slowly overshadowing and clouding out the wisdom and knowingness that was my experience prior to birth. What a shock! No wonder I didn't want to see what was before me and ended up wearing glasses at age six.

Nevertheless, here I was, and still am – the same as you reading these words. So many questions arise. Why did I want to come here? Can I really survive here for 80 years, so far removed from my connection with the Divine? Why am I slowly losing my memory of my existence beyond this world? Do I really need to be here?

Gradually, I fell into the "Maya" as the Indian mystics refer to it, or the 'Illusion' in Western terms, the same as we all do– destined to wander aimlessly in that illusion for what seems like an eternity. Or must we wander aimlessly? I contend that the wandering is not actually aimless, but only seems so because we don't know where we are going or that the imprint of a path is set before us, only we cannot see the imprint. How do we discern that imprint and learn how to follow that path? Well, that is one of the topics of this book.

In my early life, I had no idea of this. Earthly existence was a puzzle, if not a blur. Everything was so unlike where I had come from. It was loving and coarse at the same time. And there seemed to be so much that was hidden and unexpressed, but clearly felt in the interactions surrounding me.

In fact, the unexpressed was normally the most important element of that early life (and continues today) because it pointed to the fear of remembering that earlier place prior to the earthly life. In an infant body though, all I could do was experience, and make a lot of noise if I did not like the experience. Wow! That is pretty restrictive in comparison to where I had been. No wonder babies cry.

The molding forces in that time were omnipresent and my baby brain and mind completely malleable. Even if I wanted to resist, I was powerless to do so. And thus, I adopted, or more accurately conformed to, the influences surrounding me. Those influences and experiences have shaped my life since, for better or for worse, and it has taken me decades to recognize the full impact of that molding, a molding that, due to its most early influence, laid down the fundamental patterns of my life.

No wonder those earliest patterns are the most difficult to recognize. How can I be expected to recognize a pattern that has been part of me since day one? I have nothing to compare it against. It would be like trying to recognize the note that my life plays in the symphony of life. I can easily discern the notes others play. But mine? I don't even recognize that I play a note.

Same with those patterns. I can't recognize them at all. In fact, I don't even know they exist until I have a reference point with which to compare them, which is something only a matured mind can do. Is it a surprise that as a child and adolescent my behaviors were not always in line with my inner knowingness? That connection had largely been lost and I had no anchor except for those early patterns—plus patterns, beliefs, and expectations learned along the way as infancy eventually progressed to adolescence and beyond.

At the same time though—the joy of a physical experience! Playing in the dirt, holding a baby animal, laughing. All these things are not possible on the other side of life, before we take on a body. And water! For some reason, water has always been my magnet. I've never seen a waterfall that I didn't want to stand under, and have done so, for the most part.

For me, there is something magical about water. Maybe because it represents the most basic aspect of life. I don't know. But I do know that being in this world brings the opportunity to experience. And experience we do! A never-ending stream of experiences, some beneficial, others not so much.

The world is such an enigmatic place, always leading us to those new experiences, each an opportunity to contrast with the feelings we experienced earlier. Each is an opportunity to resonate, or not, with the work we are here to do. How can we know what we must glean from those experiences? How can we discern the path to follow? Sadly, our societies do not assist us well in that discernment. Guidance would certainly be valued. In the end though, the path is our own and it is our job to discern it.

My life has not been easy. No one's has, really. We don't discuss the real reason for this, though. For some reason, it is not considered socially acceptable to state that my life is hard because I know I need to move toward resolution of my separation with that place outside time and space were only God exists.

Our churches emphasize the importance of praying to God and worshiping God, but they often shy away from encouraging us to return to that connection while here in this world. We need that reconnection, however, for it rejuvenates and replenishes us. We need triggers, though, to initiate that process because we generally do not have the internal drive to initiate this process on our own. For me, this process was initiated to a great extent by living overseas.

In 1980, fresh out of college, I joined the Peace Corps and spent the next two years on an island in the Philippines. This experience blew wide open my experiences growing up in a Midwest farming community. Everything was different—the smells, the sights, the language, the climate—it was sensory overload. Most importantly though, the patterns of belief and behaviors were different.

Two years immersed in an unfamiliar culture allowed me the space to recognize the fundamental principle that each of us is a product of the culture and family in which we are raised. This was so clearly obvious during that time because I observed behaviors, and more importantly, beliefs that were totally alien to me. Not only that, but there were fundamental elements missing from this culture compared to the culture I grew up in.

A striking example of this was the near absence of sarcasm. I'll never forget my Filipino friends asking me, after they watched the movie, *On Golden Pond*, why Henry Fonda was so grumpy. In that movie he played a man who has bottled up his feelings for a lifetime, only allowing them to emerge as sarcasm. While this is a behavior I had witnessed often in American society, I was at a loss for words as to how to explain his behavior.

I came to appreciate this aspect of the Filipino culture and decided I would adopt that outlook. I didn't realize what I was taking on though, as sarcasm was a fundamental element in my family and culture for as long as I could remember. I can't say that I mastered my goal, even after forty years of effort, but I still find it to be a worthwhile pursuit.

The pattern runs so deep. This led me to explore the causes—and perhaps more importantly, the means—of resolving these unwanted patterns, a pursuit I continue to this day.

There were so many examples of how the Philippine culture deviated from my own. These came clearly into my awareness as I began to master the local language, encountering words that have no translation, or words completely missing from the English language. Sometimes entire concepts and words surrounding those concepts would be missing. A perfect example would be the concept of precision.

The Philippine dialect I learned had no words to describe fractions, other than one-half. For this reason, asking directions was always an adventure.

"How far is it to Barrio Duangan?" I would ask. The reply? "It is close," or "You are almost there," or "It is far."

So, I would ask instead, "How many kilometers to Barrio Duangan?" But generally, I would get the same response. Why? I would wonder, could I not get a clear answer to this simple question?

My engineer-trained, left-brain mind was never able to resolve that dilemma. It was clear that personal relationships and connection to nature were far more important in that culture than precision, or generally any scientific topic.

Try explaining "germ" to someone with no education living off the land in a remote mountain valley when that word does not exist in their language. I can assure you, that is no easy task.

"How is it that we can see the world so differently even though we are all living on the same planet?" I wondered.

And thus came to me my most important insight from those two years in the southeast Asian tropics. I realized just how much of a clean slate we are at birth. How our culture, society, and family shape our beliefs and patterns of interaction. How those beliefs and patterns dominate our lives, whether known or unknown.

It was then that I decided to evaluate my own patterns to determine if they were worth keeping, or if they should be discarded. What I didn't realize was that this would be a life-long effort that would take me back to my infancy. And sometimes even earlier.

2

And God said, "I never told you to believe THAT!"

Stripping away unhealthy beliefs and patterns turned out to be a far more arduous project than I had imagined. I came to see beliefs as rungs on the ladder of spiritual growth. We hold onto them tightly while climbing the ladder, and without them we would lose our stability and ultimately fall into the abyss. To find safety, we hold on tight; however, our fear of letting go prevents us from upgrading those beliefs when a clearer understanding arises.

When exposed to a new understanding, we wish to reach out to the rung representing that new perception, but we can't because our foot is still stuck on the lower rung of a belief learned in a much earlier time. Until we are willing or able to remove our foot from that lower rung, we are torn mentally and emotionally because we know we need to move forward but our fear keeps us from doing so.

Unfortunately, our culture does not give us much guidance in how to move up this ladder. You would think this would be such an important topic that it would be taught from an early age. However, it is not taught at all. Why not? I'm sure there are many reasons, but the one that stands out for me is that it raises fear for the person not willing to climb the ladder.

For example, if my son realizes that one of the beliefs I inculcated in him in his youth really wasn't healthy and he makes the effort to replace it with a healthier belief, his action creates a moment of crisis for me because now I need to evaluate my experience of that belief.

I can react wisely, honor his decision, and possibly modify my own. Or, I can react negatively and reject his movement forward. As I see it, this is at the core of much of the generational angst we see in families. This is unavoidable however, because as societies evolve, beliefs will change, hopefully in a healthy direction.

Beliefs seem to float through our lives. We are exposed to them from all directions. It is almost like walking through the cafeteria line deciding which foods to eat. Some are clearly outrageous. Others intriguing. The important action, however, is not in choosing the next delectable belief on the menu, but in letting go of the old beliefs that no longer serve us. How we can do this is another topic of this book, as there are steps that can be taken that facilitate letting loose of old beliefs and patterns.

Beliefs lie at the heart of our mental perceptions. Without them, we would have no point upon which to contrast new ideas. And, new ideas are needed to keep us engaged in the process of moving forward. More importantly, new ideas can stimulate a deeper understanding that emanates from our inner knowingness.

What is the difference between a belief and what I am referring to as inner knowingness? Let me give an example. How would you answer this question, "Is it wrong to take another's life without cause?"

Hopefully your answer is "yes," but from where does this answer originate? Is it based upon something you were taught when you were in Sunday School? Or is it something you simply "know?"

Most non-psychopathic people would simply know that to take another's life without cause is wrong, regardless of whether they learned it in Sunday School, or even if they never attended a religious training, or even if no one ever told them it was wrong. The person simply "knows" that it is wrong. No one needs to tell them.

Contrast that with a belief. For example I might say, "I believe that my country is the finest country in the world."

No matter what country one resides within, it is always possible to find some other country where an aspect of that other country's society is superior to one's own. The likely reason to hold this belief is that it was embedded in the consciousness by authority figures at an early age.

Beliefs can change with the wind, while what one "knows" is unlikely to change. In fact, what one knows is an anchor for the moral and ethical foundation of a society. Beliefs often are more of an overlay on how that knowingness is expressed.

Beliefs also serve to uphold our image of ourselves. Perhaps this is the most limiting aspect of our growth process. The strength of that image can prevent us from embracing a larger view of ourselves. Our self-image can become so entrenched that some individuals would rather take their own life than submit to changing their self-image.

The self-image embodies all the beliefs that make up its parts. It serves to hold in place our station in the world. In doing so, it provides stability. We would be lost in the world without a self-image, and yet a strictly defined self-image limits our ability to change.

Beliefs also provide us a vehicle to interact in society. Without them, we would have no point of reference. Nothing would make sense. And nothing would have meaning. We would be left wandering through our minds, desperately searching for something to hold on to, desperately searching for those rungs on the ladder.

We must choose our beliefs wisely; however, this can require much effort if our beliefs are wedded to our mental patterns, to our emotions and perhaps to our body patterns. Beliefs can foster an integration of our entire being around a single concept. For example, I might believe my life is one of a martyr. With this belief will accompany the emotional tenor of self-reproach, and my body language will align with that feeling.

While beliefs serve to uphold our self-image, it serves us to not cling to unwanted or worn-out patterns supporting those beliefs. Releasing those worn-out patterns frees our life to step into a new light, a light of understanding not previously available.

Finding an effective means of healing our belief system is an important step toward releasing our inner drive to move forward spiritually, mentally, emotionally, and even physically. How we let go of unwanted beliefs is fundamental to awakening our heart. It is our heart that urges us to unfold the deeper understanding that lies within us.

Much is said about the heart in our cultures, but seldom is the heart associated with formation, or more accurately, restructuring of beliefs. Our heart knows what beliefs will best serve us, but we need to be willing to follow that urging. To fight it creates a dissonance within us, a tension that can lead to emotional and even physical imbalance.

This internal dissonance can result from denying the need to alter a belief. This is fundamentally because beliefs provide the underlying pattern upon which much of our life is founded. Beliefs hold in place the patterns that provide structure in our lives, and without this structure, we would collapse in disarray. The beliefs must therefore be altered in a fluid way, where as one belief is released, there is a new, more profound belief waiting in the wings to replace it. In this manner, stability is maintained.

Beliefs are so fundamental to our nature and so instrumental in our social interactions that we seldom consider them. But consider them we should, for they play such an important role in living a healthy and productive life.

Lastly, beliefs serve as our grounding in a world constantly bombarding us with stimuli, much of which would upset and disorient us if we had no point of stability. Our beliefs provide stability, for they represent the nature of our deeper self that we are struggling to bring forward into the world.

Our beliefs may not initially be a clear representation of that deeper understanding, but as we move forward, gradually releasing old beliefs and replacing them with new, healthier beliefs, we move closer to a deeper understanding, to the point where we "know" truth.

This process of renewal brings an unexpected freedom, a freedom that allows us to live in an emotionally unfettered manner where assailants of all sorts attempting to undermine our stability are easily thwarted. We become steadfast—a pillar, one might say—but a flexible pillar that can change and adapt as more truth moves into our belief system and thus infuses our entire being.

Such a freedom is far more profound than freedom from political persecution or freedom from an unpleasant and restricting social situation or relationship. It can serve as a foundation of strength able to withstand the vicissitudes of life, bringing a certain peace and grounding to situations of conflict.

So much of the conflict in our society emerges from disparate beliefs. Having the skill to smoothly and flexibly grow one's belief structure greatly lubricates relationships. If all of humanity consciously strove to heal at an individual level the beliefs that bring pain and restriction to their lives, much of the world's friction would simply slip away.

Imagine a world with minimal friction. Maybe John Lennon should have added to his song, "Imagine all the people releasing old beliefs."

3

Man wondered, "Isn't there a theory to explain this?"

While it might sound wonderful to release our old beliefs and move into a healthier mode of perception and thinking, it is not obvious how to do so; therefore, it must be explained how beliefs can be altered, effectively and safely. But first we must lay some groundwork.

By groundwork, I mean an understanding of the basis for beliefs. This is a challenging topic to explore, because language is limiting and because this topic is not in the common discourse. Words enter a language slowly, and unless or until a word needs to be created to fit a concept or idea, that word does not exist. Nevertheless, I shall do my best to explain what I consider the fundamental building-blocks of a belief system and how our belief system interacts with the more obvious parts of our total being.

What follows is my perspective based upon years of contemplation and study. It provides a framework or base upon which understanding can develop. This framework can be applied to integrate the approaches and concepts discussed later in this book. It is necessary to provide such a framework so that the underlying basis of the process discussed later can take hold. The mind works best when provided a structure upon which to build. This structural framework provides that basis.

First, it should be understood that the human vehicle is built upon what is often termed the physical, emotional, mental, and spiritual levels of existence. There are levels besides these that are alluded to by those capable of perceiving them, but for understanding I will introduce only those other levels as needed for clarification. These levels of existence are all interconnected, which should be obvious since we live in a physical body and experience the other three levels, or in the case of the spiritual level, we at least have an awareness of the level.

How we perceive these levels is part of the obstacle to understanding their interrelation and interaction because we perceive them through our experience of them rather than as an outside observer. Outside observation from an independent viewpoint describes the scientific approach. But how could we make such an observation of ourselves, and how could we make such a scientific observation of others, if we do not have the technology or innate ability to perceive those levels in a manner in which they can be precisely measured? This leaves us in a quandary, because we know these levels exist.

Most of the work in this arena has focused in the area of therapy. A few researchers such as Wilhelm Reich, the HeartMath Institute, and others have attempted to quantify these relationships and interactions with varying degrees of success. Most notably, the HeartMath Institute has focused on the central role played by the heart in this interaction. Their work constitutes some of the most important and leading-edge research relating to stress, heart intelligence, positive emotions, and much more.

The goal of this discussion, however, is to describe the interactions and relationships more from a spiritual and energetic perspective. It is useful to understand the building-blocks and interrelationships of those building-blocks if one is to actively transform and upgrade one's persona. Software upgrade is a good analogy for this work.

We can't see, touch, or hear software, and yet it allows our computer to perform functions. As we improve the software, the computer becomes more capable of performing a greater range of functions. If the software is well written, the computer not only performs more functions but does so in a smoother fashion, one that avoids errors and prevents computer crashes.

The concept of a software upgrade is an insightful analogy to upgrading our beliefs and patterns. To bring the analogy to life, we must learn how to "program" our own internal code.

Our internal code presents itself as a wide array of energetic impulses, all moving with their own frequencies. Blending and harmonizing these frequencies lessens the friction between these energetic impulses and smooths the overall internal interaction. These interactions rely upon guidance from our higher source to achieve harmony, but that is not a direct level of control.

A direct level of control would bypass the fundamental free will we are given while living in this multi-part human vehicle effectively separated from that enlightened part of our self, often termed the higher self.

Our higher self is like the orchestra conductor who guides the orchestra by picturing in his or her mind the blending of the orchestral sounds without overtly directing the orchestra. The orchestra members must become attuned to the conductor's mind, upon which they can begin to play at his or her level of understanding. In this example, the orchestra members must learn to resonate with the conductor's mental frequency. Until the orchestra members learn to do this, the music is played, but it will not be the intended harmonic symphony.

Learning to play our instrument in tune with our higher self is a lifetime's work. In fact, it is the work of many lifetimes, for such a grand goal cannot be learned in only one lifetime, especially when we are working with a physical body operating at a frequency level much below that of the higher self. Learning to facilitate this connection and resonance is possible by allowing the lower frequencies of the physical, emotional, and mental levels to attune to the pattern set by the higher self. It is as if the higher self strikes a tone, and this tone remains a steadfast beacon toward which all other levels will eventually resonate, or at least harmonize.

Aligning with the higher self—and thus with our purpose in the world—requires allowing resonance with the higher self's tone at all levels of our manifest being. This is not a forced process. It happens naturally if allowed and supported. It would automatically occur without our interference. Much of that interference, however, is not of our making.

Interference is fundamental to living a physical existence inside a time-space continuum. Living in the physical world produces a condition of restricted frequency. While living a physical life, we are trapped in matter.

Matter can be thought of as energy trapped in time and space. This can be recognized by qualitative analysis of Einstein's equation $E=mc^2$, where E = energy, m = mass or matter, and c = the speed of light. The vibration level is limited by the frequency of light.

Beyond the physical plane, this limitation does not exist because at those higher levels, such as the emotional and mental, the "matter" comprising those levels is bound by different constraints and different mathematical relationships. We have not yet scientifically discovered those relationships, nor have we scientifically identified the "matter" at these levels. In time humanity will explore these realms, and in the process gain a deeper understanding.

For this discussion, though, let's assume that we accept matter, or a fundamental building-block, exists on the emotional level and on the mental level, since these are the primary focus of discussion. How we look at this concept defines our understanding of it, so let's consider a particle of that matter as a pebble on a beach. The pebble is constantly moved by the waves. When the tide is out, the pebble is still. When the tide is in, the pebble is moving. When a storm is present, the pebble is churned about.

This analogy illustrates matter on the emotional plane where the energy in the waves represents the mental impulses arising in our mind. Emotions generally accompany thoughts, which then enhance the strength of the emotion. If the same thought continues repeatedly, the pebble constantly moves back and forth in the same pattern or location. If the movement of the pebble is fluid, it experiences little resistance with its neighboring pebbles. If the movement of the pebble is abrasive, its churning upsets the nearby pebbles.

So it is with our emotional matter. When our emotions are fluid, their propensity is to avoid upset. This is not in reference to any particular emotion, but instead to the tone of the emotion, for the tone can be either harmonious or abrasive. How we approach accessing our emotional storehouse determines how that storehouse is expressed.

People who unceremoniously express their emotions neglect responsibility for their emotional "pebbles" and as a result, their pebbles are thrown about and have abrasive interactions with the emotional pebbles of others. Others will experience this as an emotional upset, particularly when the abrasive push of the pebbles from the upset individual carry enough energy to begin to move the pebbles of the recipient out of their normal pattern. This is described in common conversation as someone's behavior "wearing" on another, which is accurate when the constant abrasive movement of one is continuously impinging upon the emotional substance of the other.

Another situation where this arises is where one holds their emotional substance too tightly. We refer to this as someone having "bottled up" their emotions. Again, our vernacular expression correctly captures the conditions. Let loose of the cork, and all the emotional substance spews forth under pressure, impacting the emotional substance of anyone in a position to be impacted. We have all seen and experienced this interaction. The violent nature of the release can have such an impact that it can leave a recipient feeling physically ill.

Why would this interaction cause physical illness? Because the nature of emotional substance is such that it flushes out resonant physical atoms and molecules. In the case of feelings of discomfort, this is typically associated with emotional substance of lower vibration. Associated with these lower vibrations are physical atoms and associated molecules that are dissonant with a healthy state of the body.

These dissonant molecules break loose and flush out to be eliminated, essentially creating a toxin release. The physical feeling is comparable to having the flu. I know this because I have experienced such a response many times after a period of emotional release. That is why holistic health practitioners always advising drinking a lot of water following any type of energetic or emotional healing work. This is also why it is useful to drink lots of water following a good massage.

We should not confuse vibrational frequency with the force causing movement of emotional substance. Emotional intensity relates to the force with which emotional substance can move. Emotional frequency relates to the specific type of emotion. This is why in metaphysical studies, body parts and body systems are associated with specific emotions or with specific emotional patterns. This also explains the function of frequency-based diagnostic machines, pioneered by Royal Raymond Rife, a gifted scientist and inventor in the early twentieth century. Others have copied Rife's ideas, developing similar machines that are used today.

These machines are capable of measuring frequencies in the body. Those frequencies can be correlated to specific types of cells, and with enough fine tuning, can be correlated to specific emotional states. I have used one called the Asyra, and found it accurate at diagnosing a number of conditions of which I was already aware. It also diagnosed a condition I did not know I had, but was confirmed later by standard medical testing. I use its results as another data point when evaluating my health condition.

Once science learns how to quantify emotional substance and begins to measure its quantity and frequency, the function of these machines will become clear, and be advanced to a very beneficial state for the emotional and mental health of those utilizing this technology.

Resonance with yet other fields within the body leads the recipient of an emotional interaction into yet other energetic experiences. In particular, resonance with the intermediate layer I shall refer to as the "pattern layer" plays an important role in defining our physical health. The nascent field of epigenetics provides a rudimentary understanding of this pattern layer.

Epigenetics theory states that the DNA expression can be modified through means other than physical interaction, even though the DNA chain itself is strictly physical. This is so due to the existence of the pattern underlying physical molecules. This pattern functions similar to a magnetic field.

Place a bar magnet under a piece of paper with iron filings on top of the paper. Shake the paper and the iron filings will align themselves to conform with the pattern of the magnetic field. DNA operates in a similar fashion, being supported and defined by an underlying pattern at the pattern level.

The pattern level is in a sense a mediator between the emotional/mental levels and the physical level. Both emotions and thoughts can affect the pattern, especially when focused over a long period of time. The influence can be for enhanced functionality, or for degeneration. The DNA does not recognize the direction, only the influence.

If the thought or emotion is destructive in nature, the DNA can be damaged over time. This is classically seen in cancer, where the DNA has been damaged in a way that its natural cell death (apoptosis) process has been turned off. Thus the cell does not die as would normally be the case and instead reproduces new cells with the same mutation, resulting in a proliferation of cancer cells that eventually engulf the entire body, causing it to die.

Of course, cancer can also be triggered by physical stimuli, but without the destructive thought or emotion affecting the DNA pattern, the DNA will be less likely to succumb to the physical or chemical influence causing the damage. Even if physical damage is induced, if the emotional and mental frequency is at a high level, the immune system will be triggered to attack and remove the cancerous cells.

Without a clear direction, the mind would affect the DNA in a potentially deleterious manner, resulting in disease. Fortunately, a natural barrier exists between the mental substance and the pattern level. This natural barrier acts as a buffer, preventing instantaneous changes at the pattern level. The same is true for substance at the emotional level. It is necessary that this be so, otherwise the DNA would be jerked to and fro, rendering it unstable.

Unstable DNA as a normal condition would be detrimental to the physical body and undermine the goal of allowing a human experience. Nevertheless, the DNA can be affected by thoughts and emotions, although generally over a long timeframe. Dissonance in the mental and emotional substance creates, over time, a distortion at the pattern level, and in time this distortion creates, through resonance, a distortion at the physical level.

Of course, this effect can also work to our advantage. By raising the vibration level of our thoughts or emotions, we can influence the pattern guiding the DNA to evolve, analogous to how software evolves during revision. The higher vibration can influence the pattern to twist, fold, expand, or "flower" into new forms where their beauty resonates with the higher-frequency thought forms or higher-frequency emotions.

This "flowering" is impactful because it represents new features in the pattern, features that may represent information gained in other lifetimes and possibly even on other worlds and different body types carried forth in the pattern. When operating at this level of creation—the fundamental manner in which evolution occurs in the animal and plant kingdoms—changes to the DNA are natural and in harmony with natural principle. Contrast that with genetic modification using brute-force alteration of the DNA strands at the physical level.

This brute-force method creates life forms out of harmony with the natural order, creating a potentially unstoppable dilemma should the new life form turn out to be dominant or damaging, or both. Genetic modification should only be performed using techniques nature has provided based on the wisdom of the Creator. To do otherwise violates the Creator's plan and brings potential for disaster at the physical level. The DNA modification method provided by nature is fail-safe, because if the modification is one of dissonance, that is, based on a negative thought or emotion, the result is damage to the DNA and eventual death of the cell, of the host, or both. Alterations to DNA should only occur using the approach outlined here if the result is to be truly beneficial and long lasting.

Imagine the progress a race could make if, instead of using various technologies to enhance the life of its individual members, the enhancements were made at the DNA level by steadily raising the frequency of the mental and emotional substance? Not only can this improve the health of the body, but as discussed earlier, the elevated vibrations lubricate the movement of the mental and emotional substance between individuals.

In an enlightened society or race, focus on these higher vibrations produces a steady spiral upward of advancement, leading to abilities and a quality of life only imagined in our current existence. The human race is far from achieving this state, but doing so is a worthy goal to pursue. In doing so, not only would quality of life be enhanced, but the discord present today would naturally fall away.

Much of this discord is exacerbated by the dissonant vibrations found in modern society. Raucous noises are one example of this. Noise that is out of harmony with one's emotional frequencies produces a reaction in the physical body similar to the reaction of a wave that crashes onto the rocks. In doing so, this noise causes perturbations in the underlying structures that result in dissonance. It is this dissonance that creates the imbalance at the emotional level.

In a sense, the noise vibrates the "pebbles" mentioned earlier outside their normal range of movement. We experience this as an emotional upset. There are many other examples of influences that can lead to emotional upset. Another example is the experience of being in a crowd of people caught up in an emotional response. It is difficult to maintain one's emotional stability in such a situation because the flow of everyone's emotional substance is moving in a common direction. Add to that its intensity, and the emotion becomes contagious, creating the oft-termed "mob mentality."

To achieve a state of internal and external harmony, a society or race must learn to ameliorate the impact of these influences. The first step is to understand their impact. Without understanding their impact, it becomes more difficult to overcome the influence.

If a machine were available to show how one's emotional nature is influenced by impacts such as noise or emotional state of others, then the picture would be clear. Of course, it is true that soothing and inspiring sounds can have a beneficial effect. Long-term exposure to uplifting music can lead to the alternate effect by bringing alignment at the pattern level and gradually creating a more holistic arrangement. Since DNA conforms to the enhanced pattern, alignment can lead to improved health benefits. While improved health is not the only positive impact of such influences, it is an important one.

Other impacts of importance are related to how the body interacts with the messages received at a cellular level from the DNA. These messages arrive at an electrochemical level, but also at a deeper level that provides important messages designed to bring the physical body substance into alignment with the pattern level. In this way, optimal health can be achieved in the physical body.

4

God replied, "Why are you so uptight?"

In today's world the drive to excel is ever present. It can lead us to great levels of achievement, but it can also lead us to undermine our basic calmness. This drive creates a level of tension designed to move us forward. How we approach this tension is fundamental to our experience in the world.

Tension is a necessary element of life. It can lead us to great achievements or it can cause us to experience discord. Tension in the human vehicle is similar to tension in the bow when shooting an arrow. Without tension, there is no movement forward. How we release the tension is what matters.

The most effective means of releasing tension is to allow it to suffuse the entire body, rather than hold it in a specific location. If held in a specific location, the energy becomes blocked and the creativity associated with the tension, or perhaps, the driving force behind the tension is blocked. I am speaking of the inner tension that causes us to move forward, the tension that motivates us to achieve in life. Other tensions exist as a result of daily living but these are easily manageable if the inner tension is understood and effectively released.

Tension is expressed in our lives in many ways. If expressed effectively, it will show up as a smooth impetus moving us forward. In this role, it is positive in our lives, for it motivates us to grow and achieve. Everyone has this inner tension, although it is more prevalent in some than in others. It is important to embark upon a process designed to facilitate, manage, and utilize this tension.

I am an example of this tension. It has been present in me since an early age. I remember waking up in bed as a young boy watching the dust particles float in the air, reflected by the morning sun as it streamed through the window, thinking, "I must get up and move. I need to do something." In later years, that tension built. I always felt a need to "do something." I am sure now it irritated some of my acquaintances. I couldn't really control it, for it was such a driving force. Numerous people have spoken to me of it over the years and how I push myself. I find it to be less prevalent now. I attribute that to years of Tai Chi practice, followed by years of serious illness.

Until a process to manage and utilize this tension is undertaken in earnest and some success achieved, it will plague us as we move through the challenges of our temporary existence in the human form.

Those who have learned to manage it effectively have discovered that they can harness its force and reach great achievements. This is possible for everyone; however, many will find it challenging, in part because no awareness or training is provided for the role of tension or how to successfully harness its force. To successfully do so, one must let go of preconceived ideas of how tension arises.

We are born with this inner tension, regardless of what influences we might experience in our growth and development that would either enhance it or properly channel it. Our relationship to this inner tension teaches us how to manage daily tensions. If we let go of our ideas about success, the anchor holding the tension is loosened. This releases the tension, allowing our natural vibration to express. The heart plays the essential role in calming and properly channeling our tension for productive means.

Without the balancing role of the heart, the tension would overwhelm us and disrupt our emotional and physical bodies. Fortunately, there are methods by which the tension can be calmed. For example, if one focuses on the heart and breathes in and out of the heart, an alignment is created between the power of the heart and the pattern layer. This gives the heart dominance over the pattern layer, and in effect dominance over the DNA and all that is impacted and controlled by the DNA.

How the heart performs this function is not readily apparent in our medical evaluations, but it is well embedded in the vernacular language by such phrases as "heartfelt" and "heartache." These phrases reflect the inherent understanding that the heart is directly connected to the emotional nature, and as discussed earlier, the emotional nature directly impacts the physical.

The heart is such an important feature in the human experience. It is far more than the physical heart. The studies of the HeartMath Institute have provided important research illustrating this. The heart is designed at the pattern and energetic levels to support a solid connection with the Divine. In this way it balances the sometimes raucous happenings in the emotional and physical body. Living heart-centered is not just a catch phrase, for it has relevance to this connection.

The heart feeds signals to the emotional body that are capable of fully overpowering the emotional nature, bringing a calmness that is unachievable otherwise in a turbulent world. It behooves us to tap into this heart-based control. Heart-based control is important because it allows overriding the mind. The mind can be easily upset and sometimes aberrant, but the heart, due to its divine connection, is stable. It cannot be perturbed. It can only be ignored.

Unfortunately in current society, the heart *is* often ignored. The divine connection to the heart is what produces inner tension, because it infuses the entire being with a force field that energizes the mental, emotional, and physical substances continuously. This force field creates a base of operation, without which the body would simply die.

Death is more a function of the heart's force field retracting from the human body and returning to the divine. Once the heart removes its force, the body shuts down. The heart is such a magnificent gift. Little is really known scientifically about its complete role and capabilities.

The heart carries memory and in a sense, has its own brain. As with the larger human brain, the heart's brain can be programmed to serve an individual. The heart is also a repository of goodwill.

The goodwill to which I refer is specifically that arriving through the divine connection. One might call it grace, but the goodwill to which I refer is actually an energetic substance, whereas grace is more of a spiritual impetus. The two can go hand-in-hand. Grace is ever available, though, and its passageway is through the heart.

The heart serves to smoothly release inner tension in the human vehicle in a balanced way. Without this balance, the inner tension distributes unevenly. The heart allows the inner tension to seep into the emotional substance gradually, thus calming it. If the heart is stopped from doing this, the tension arriving in the body, as well as the tension coming from daily living, can collide and build up in susceptible areas

This buildup coalesces emotional substance in its midst, and in turn influences the physical substance. For this reason, the tension buildup is felt physically. One can work backward to release the tension by massage or other treatment to the physical location, or by emotional release. Both of these can be effective. Ultimately, the heart is needed to clear the tension and permanently remove it. Tools, such as meditation, are available to achieve this result.

Meditation is a successful approach because it serves to align the spiritual level of the being with the heart and in so doing aligns with the divine. Meditation or prayer can be very powerful in this role for they both perform at the same level, providing the prayer isn't the type of just asking for something. Prayer should be in the form of alignment with the divine, and in that way is fundamentally no different than meditation.

How the heart performs its functions is mysterious—yet understandable. It places itself at the center of the body so that it can most effectively influence all areas.

The most challenging role performed by the heart is in relation to the mind, for the mind is like an undisciplined child. It flits here and there, not easily focused on any one thing, but enamored by the next shiny object. If anything needs stabilization by the heart, it is the mind; however, the mind is seldom interested in being stabilized or disciplined. It simply wants to be left alone and allowed to rule an individual's life. This is obviously not a desirable approach toward living. If the mind is allowed to operate unchecked, it will be prone to all sorts of mischief, mischief that can cause damage at many levels.

At a deeper level, though, the mind prefers discipline. The heart is perfectly situated to provide such discipline, for the heart has the ability to create order and stability in the mental substance. Mental stability is necessary for emotional and physical stability. If the mental impetus is unruly, the emotions will become unruly, and over time, the physical body will be negatively affected.

The heart can directly feed the mind information it cannot otherwise acquire. The mind is part of our animal-based vehicle, and as such has developed over eons of time and through often treacherous situations. The hunt for survival in those early days developed an entrenched fear thought form. While fear is necessary for survival in dangerous situations, it is not desirable as a dominant mode of thinking, and yet it remains that way for many people.

Fear can block the impetus from the heart more than any other thought form or emotion. As a result, the heart is most challenged when the mind is fixated on fear. Fear is seen as a thought/emotion but it needs to be seen as a pattern. It is the pattern that creates havoc.

So, what needs to be done to release this pattern? First, realize that fear is an inherent pattern in the human vehicle due to its carry-over from the earlier time. It is helpful to recognize existence of an unhealthy pattern because that allows the mind to focus on releasing it. The more ingrained the pattern, the harder it is to release. Imagine a pattern that has existed for millennia and how entrenched it must be.

Fear is not the only pattern of this sort, but it is one of the most pernicious because it so effectively blocks the heart's influence from the rest of the human vehicle. Without fear, the essence flowing from the heart can sustain a balanced level of comfort in the body. It is this comfort that allows tension to diminish by distributing it evenly throughout the body.

Why is release of tension so important? Because tension buildup in parts of the body restricts the flow of life force—what in Taoism is called chi. Releasing this tension dissolves the locked-in patterns holding us back.

No surprise—it is difficult to be in a physical body. Our spirit is one with the divine, yet we are separated from the divine, inhabiting an animal body with limited abilities, struggling with carried-over, animal-based patterns that prevent us from sensing our divine connection. This separation in itself creates great tension, but as with all tension, the age-old patterns are worn down through the inexorable flow of divine essence feeding through the heart. This ingenious design allows us to eventually and gradually re-experience connection with the divine while inhabiting a physical body.

In essence, the heart is the key to resolving tension, and as such, much of the conflict and dissension in the world. The heart, over time, will dominate the human experience, even if this takes many lifetimes.

5

Man asked, "How do we access this heart essence?"

Heart essence is accessed through intention and practice. The heart must first be recognized as the central feature for living a fulfilling life. By living in connection with the heart, we are able to overcome most of the hindrances to our growth and development. How this occurs should not be as mysterious as it is made out to be. I know from my own experience practicing Tai Chi for many years that by accessing the heart essence (among other things), this discipline can bring balance to the human experience at all levels.

Practice can take many forms. In our lifetimes we are exposed to a multitude of experiences, many of which are designed to provide us opportunities to access the heart connection. To focus on that connection is the key. Again, it is largely a matter of intent. With intent, the mind is focused and in alignment with the heart.

Intent is set in the mind. The mind enjoys operating with intent because this gives it structure and focus. The mind prefers a structured experience; however, the unruly mental patterns developed over millennia often collide with the intentions set by following the heart.

In this picture, the heart can be seen as a humming generator. It constantly feeds the system a transformed version of the divine essence in a form the other three bodies – mental, emotional, and physical can access and utilize. Without this generator the other bodies would be in disarray, lacking in focus and vitality. Combining the generated heart essence with intent of the mind creates a powerful tool for transformation, a tool that can over time dissolve the entrenched patterns in the mind. The result of this is FREEDOM.

Inner freedom is a primary goal in life. Release from entrapping patterns, the strongest originating in infancy, is a powerful experience that can lead to unexpected realizations and much welcome relief. This result is consistent with the function of the heart, for the heart is fundamentally free. It is an expression of the Divine that knows no restriction. It is the mind that creates restriction.

Once unfettered by restriction from unhealthy and blocking patterns, the heart can suffuse the three bodies with an energy and regulation that brings stability and peace. This inner peace feeds back on the overall process to allow breakdown of unwanted patterns at all levels at an accelerating rate. While these unhealthy patterns may no longer be desirable, they were needed at one time, so they can be blessed and released. The substance previously trapped in their boundaries is now available for use in more important endeavors. More importantly, the heart is now freed to spread its "goodwill" further throughout the entire system. The acceleration of this process represents a magnificent turning point in one's life.

So, how can one achieve this level of internal freedom? Intent is always a primary factor, but beyond intent, there are positive actions one can take. For example, focusing on the heart in order to align with its essence is fundamental to accessing that essence.

Again, this can be done through meditation or prayer, or through techniques such as those offered by the HeartMath Institute.

Feeling through your heart the Presence of another provides another path for achieving this freedom. We all know what it means to feel another's "vibe," but I am talking about the divine presence of another, which is more than the vibration at a mental or emotional level. The divine essence of another's Presence and the emotional vibe are harmonics of one another, where the vibe is modified by expression through the human vehicle.

Sensing the Presence of another is a learned ability even though it can arise spontaneously at times. One way it shows itself is as an awareness of that person's potential, in contrast to that person's personality. How we interpret the experience of another's expression filters our own, allowing us to better evaluate the interaction between us. In a healthy interaction, the emotional barriers between two people that can block awareness of the divine presence are minimized, allowing a deeper connection.

Resonance between two people is largely a result of the fundamental vibration at the level of the heart. This vibration is naturally modified by the personality and body type. When severe blocking patterns are present in either or both individuals, the heart essence cannot be expressed purely. Unless the two individuals have resonance between their blocking patterns, there is dissonance, emotional upset, negative thoughts, etc., between them.

As we progress down the path of pattern release, the heart essence becomes ever more apparent to others. With someone who has released many of the debilitating patterns, experience of someone's heart essence is like a reunion. For someone struggling with difficult blocking patterns, experience of another's heart essence can produce a range of emotions and responses because it serves to dislodge those patterns in the receiver. This occurs through sharing of the mental and emotional substance, and is more pronounced if physical contact is also involved. This is the method by which great teachers and healers can initiate growth and healing in their students even if they are not in physical contact, and even at remote distances. Such is the power of the heart in combination with the mental and emotional substance. Mental substance is not constrained by time and space.

In healing our dysfunctional patterns we must first recognize that we are not at fault for their creation. Some were adopted at birth while others were formed by family and society as we grew and experienced the world. The patterns we inherited at birth existed in the energy bodies of our parents and were carried over to our bodies. At the physical level, this is an aspect of epigenetics.

Epigenetics describes how our environment affects our genetic expression; however, epigenetics as it is currently viewed does not account for the carryover of emotional and mental substance and associated patterns from parent to child. These substances and patterns, while not as influential as learned patterns, are still very influential. We see this in adopted children who grow up having some of the mental and emotional patterns of their biological parents.

Realization of this carry-over can be of great benefit for someone embarking upon the path to inner freedom because not only does the understanding arise that they are not at fault for some of their urges and undesirable behaviors, but they can recognize those patterns and influences and at a mental level work to dissolve them. In my own experience, evaluating these patterns was an important step forward.

At one point in my life I decided to evaluate the characteristics and patterns of both of my parents. I listed on a piece of paper the characteristics I admired and also the characteristics and behaviors I did not find useful. I then focused on the desirable characteristics and in my mind thanked them for providing that gift. I also set a goal to release the undesirable characteristics and worked for many years to do so. Through this process, I developed a greater compassion for my parents (who were alive at the time), and in my experience a deeper relationship with them.

Because I had known all four of my grandparents, I did the same process with them, evaluating their strengths and weaknesses and seeing clearly how their patterns had affected my parents and thus me. This is the most important healing activity in which I ever engaged in regard to my family and through it I experienced great compassion not just for my parents, but also for my grandparents. I imagined what my grandparent's lives must have been like and what formed their life experience.

Through meditation, I carried this process even further back to more remote ancestors, sensing patterns carried over for at least a century and perhaps much longer. I let go of those patterns as best I could by setting an intention and then allowing release. Many times, I would physically place my hands where the pattern seemed to be lodged and imagine releasing the trapped substance or pattern from the location. Surprisingly, I found this process to be effective, even at times leading to tears of joy when the pattern was released.

A teacher of mine had taught me this method and I found it very useful. I use it to this day. It helps to state with intention, "I give every cell of my body permission to release XXX," or "I give every aspect of my three-part body permission to release XXX," where XXX is the no-longer-desired emotion, illness, thought, or underlying pattern. I found this technique can be powerful, even to the point that doing this could initiate a release capable of making me physically ill. I learned, therefore, to take care using it and first ask if it was safe to do this release, or if I should wait until a later time.

Another teacher recommended I leave these released energy forms and patterns nearby so I could thank them for their role in my life, and when I was finished thanking them, I should release them completely from my life. My mental image was to place them in a rectangular bucket in front of me, then after an appropriate number of days I would imagine throwing them into the lava flow or Mordor. Not sure why I picked Mordor, but it certainly melted the energy forms, at least in my mind.

This has been a very effective technique for me in releasing patterns over the years – at least patterns not so stubbornly stuck that I can release them on my own. Other patterns are simply too ingrained and require the help of a trained healer. One significant instance of this for me relates to the twisted pelvis I have had since infancy.

I was born with a condition called spondylolisthesis, which is a condition where the lower spine is not fully formed. This has caused chronic back ache for decades and I have tried unsuccessfully to release the tension and underlying pattern for years. As is the case with these situations though, the time came when the pattern was ready to be released.

In this instance, I required the help of an energy healer whom I dearly love and admire. She has helped me tremendously when I am stuck. In this instance, while she was working with me, I had a clear image of myself as an infant, maybe two years old, standing next to a wall with my hip hurting, probably soon after I learned to walk. I understood that to compensate, I learned to twist my pelvis to alleviate the pain. I had a tremendous release of trapped energy; accompanied by lots of deep sobs and crying, as is typically the case.

This was a more interesting case for me than most pattern release of this sort because the pattern had been ingrained in me from such an early age and also was present physically. The pattern was so close to who I am that I was unable to recognize its existence for decades. I'm sure I had needed to release numerous unhealthy patterns earlier to arrive at the point where this one could be released—since it took sixty years to resolve. Not surprisingly, my chronic back issues reduced considerably after that. I still have chronic issues in that area, but it is not as prevalent as before.

I believe the technique I have described here can work well for anyone in releasing old patterns, although I recommend soliciting the help of an accomplished healer or teacher when starting out, as he or she can teach you how the experience feels. Once you learn how it feels, you can practice it on yourself.

FINDING INNER FREEDOM

I have utilized many teachers and healers along the way and I certainly couldn't have progressed without them. I can't say I am anything special, but I can say that over the decades I have let go of many of the old patterns, emotions, and feelings in my body that plagued me before. In fact, I think this decade's long process is what has prompted me to write this book. I'd like to think that because of that process, I'm able to let my heart essence flow through to express itself on the page.

6

God asked "Why do you beat yourself up so much?"

So many things in our lives keep us from achieving the freedom to which I refer – our busy lives, struggle to succeed, time commitments, expectations of others; the list goes on and on. We must set aside some time to tackle the imbalances in our lives. Without setting aside time, preferably in a peaceful setting, it is difficult to do the work I have described. Setting aside time can lead to a regular practice that will over time produce the desired result. It requires discipline. It also requires encouragement because others may not appreciate your attempts at release.

I was blessed by living for thirty years associated with the intentional community of Stelle, Illinois, where for many years there was considerable focus on this type of work. Furthermore, there were numerous spiritual teachers and healers who visited the community to share their gifts with anyone willing to partake. I am grateful for that opportunity and did my best to access these gifts as my time allowed.

FINDING INNER FREEDOM

In subsequent decades such teachers and healers have become more prevalent in general society than they were when I started in this work. This is beneficial to anyone wanting to walk that path. Of course, discretion is advised because many self-promoting healers may not be as skilled. In my experience, the healers I have found the most powerfully effective were self-effacing and never promoted themselves as having special talents. These are the ones I would look for, but you can't know them until you have worked with them a time or two.

Somewhere along this path it is important to take notice of your progress. If you do not evaluate your progress you are likely to ignore past successes and focus on the obstacles ahead, potentially leading to discouragement that may deter further progress. Keep a journal to track your achievements and inner experiences for later review.

Feelings of inadequacy along the path are to be expected. I have felt for years that I will never finish releasing undesirable patterns and behaviors I embody. Most likely, I won't release them all, but that is no excuse for not trying. The freedom achieved by release of undesirable and unhealthy patterns is hard to describe. I know I am not the person I was forty years ago – none of us really are, but at this point, I cannot recall what it felt like to be in my body then.

So much has changed gradually over the years. Did I have more aches and pains than I have now? Did I have more mental and emotional angst than I have now? I suspect I had more then, but the human condition has a way of blocking out pain such that it is not debilitating and overpowering. It is good that is so because many people in the world live in so much emotional pain that if they were suddenly to experience all of it at once, they might lose their minds.

Release of pain caused by blocked and dysfunctional patterns is one of the greatest gifts life can give. In doing so, the heart essence described earlier can flow evenly throughout the entire human vehicle; allowing health to return at all levels. Is this easy to achieve? No. That is why we need many, many lifetimes to work all of this out.

This may seem insurmountable considering that we must, in each new lifetime, incarnate into a new body fraught with all its limitations, but in reality, the wisdom learned through many reincarnations is carried into the next, providing a pathway for connecting with the divine, regardless of the body into which one incarnates. How can this be? What we think of as the soul carries this information with it from incarnation to incarnation, building as it goes.

The soul lies at a different energetic level somewhere between the divine and the human vehicle. You could think of it as a repository from which the heart can draw upon when feeding divine essence into the three-part vehicle of the mental, emotional, and physical bodies. The Soul can provide impetus, or perhaps you might think of it as a flavoring, to the heart's essence. In doing so, it facilitates awakening of the substances in the three-part vehicle in a manner that would be more difficult than if the soul were less developed.

This awakening supports an increased pace of one's development because the individual feels an awareness of the past experience carried over in the soul, and advanced individuals can directly experience the prior learned wisdom. This is a great advantage for development, and explains why some people are more naturally advanced along the path.

The path of spiritual evolution is a continuum. We are all somewhere on that continuum. It matters not where we are, though, for eventually we all will completely reconnect with the Creator, although that will not occur in the physical reality because of the limitations of the time-space continuum.

Reconnection is the ultimate goal, but it takes many lifetimes. We are drawn to the Creator through mysterious forces. It is as if we were small iron blocks buried within an onion, and the Creator was an omnipresent, irresistible magnet suffusing the entire universe. The onion layers obstruct God's magnetic pull, and the greater the number of layers, lesser is the pull.

Our goal while physically embodied is to peel the onion layers by letting go of what blocks us from experiencing the Creator. In doing so, we gradually strengthen our connection, and as it grows and the layers recede, desire grows for complete reconnection.

In a grander sense, the blockages placed before us are a gift because they allow us to experience the contrast of being disconnected consciously with the Creator. Before birth, when we are on the other side of life, we do not experience this disconnection, so to have a true appreciation of the splendor of the Creator, we place a translucent veil between us and the Creator by being born into physical existence. Those desiring deeper separation choose more layers.

This process reminds me of my issue of living with pelvic dysfunction for many decades. Because it was so much a part of my conscious existence in this lifetime, I was unaware of the source of the pain. Now that I have released it, at least to a certain extent, I can experience the contrast of freedom in that area vs. a lifetime of chronic pain.

To continue down this path requires a generally positive outlook. That is not to say that one needs to try to be happy all the time. Happiness is more a state of instantaneous joy, whereas positive outlook is a state of underlying joy constantly bubbling up to infuse one's life. Therefore, positive outlook is of great value.

I have struggled greatly finding joy, especially in light of serious illness. There is nothing more effective at suppressing one's positive outlook than having a serious illness. In my case, it was a benign pituitary gland tumor. This significantly disrupted my hormone production. I joke about it as having gone through menopause at an order of magnitude higher. I am largely recovered now after having the tumor removed, but during the multi-year recovery process, restoring and balancing my hormones has been very challenging.

I tried to use the hormonal imbalance as an opportunity for growth, specifically for releasing old unwanted patterns. The pituitary controls nearly all the glands in the body, and in my case nearly all my glands were off-kilter. Some, such as the thyroid and adrenal, can make life very difficult if they are not working properly.

I took this as an opportunity to address multiple unhealthy patterns at the same time. Because so many of my glands were affected at once, it was as if I had multiple diseases at once, each reflecting a different frequency/pattern, and therefore each having different issues to resolve. I felt like I was in a constant healing crisis . It was not fun, but you know what they say about when life brings lemons. In the end, I benefited from an internal growth standpoint because I was forced to let go of my ego in many ways, especially adopting a humility that was in contrast to my earlier arrogance.

Before the tumor, most things in life had come relatively easy to me – work, school, sports, etc.—because I could use my will to overcome any obstacles. However, when it comes to health, will power is not the operative tool. I found that release, and ultimately humility toward my now delicate human condition, was far more effective. My health crisis was certainly rooted in unhealthy patterns of my past. The pattern that stands out most egregiously was the idea learned at an early age that I needed to be useful and help others in order to be accepted.

We all learn a coping method for surviving in life. My coping method was "helpfulness," in order to be accepted and avoid conflict. Being unaware of the detrimental nature of this pattern if carried to the point that my needs are not protected, I ran face first into its consequences. It took me a number of years before I realized that this was a major cause of my dis-ease, for I had let others use and manipulate me, all the while thinking that the activities in which I was engaged with them were beneficial to them. I thought I was tough enough to take it, but I now see that I had allowed and enabled treatment that was abusive to my health and well-being. I awoke to a nearly ten-year healing process that completely redirected my life, a healing process I still struggle with today because my thyroid and adrenal glands have become so sensitive to any amount of stress.

Looking back on my experience, I have sometimes been grateful because had I not been ill, I probably would not have embarked on a deeper stage of my inner journey of cleansing and release. My health is not perfect today, but at least I am now more aware of the work I must do to find an acceptable level of health.

Hopefully others do not need to take the path of a challenged health system, but it is not uncommon for us to bring serious challenges into our lives that spur us to achieve a greater sense of wholeness. Such serious situations are often necessary to wake us from our slumber. I thought I was already working in the direction of release and healing prior to the tumor, but it turned out that the path I was on was not going to achieve the result desired by my higher self, or at least not in the desired amount of time.

Perhaps my story can assist others in addressing the underlying healing they need to master to find a fuller and more complete life. Of interest to me in my entire episode is that outwardly I probably looked and seemed the same to those who know me, but inwardly was a different story. I feel a bit naked here because I rarely talk to anyone about this, and here I am sharing it with the world.

To summarize my experience, I needed to let go of my need to master any challenge and to a certain extent give myself over to life in a way that was unfamiliar to me. My mind and will are not the only controlling aspects of my existence and there is no advantage to being hard on myself for being ill or for not being whom I thought society wanted me to be. I have never felt I fit very well into the world, and certainly have had challenges fitting into the American work ethic.

As an amusing side, some of my work has carried me to China to teach classes. As preparation for teaching those classes, I completed a cultural questionnaire intended to assess my cultural leanings, the cultures in which I could most easily work, and the cultures in which I would have the most difficulty working. Ironically, the questionnaire determined that I was best suited to work with Filipinos and least suited to work with Americans. I had to laugh at that, because the fun-loving Filipinos I know represent my right-brain expression while the hard-working Americans I engage with represent my left-brain activities. Since my wife is Filipina, I normally engage with both.

7

But Man complained, "Why is this so hard?"

L iving an earthly life is not easy, but it doesn't need to be dreadful. Many find it largely enjoyable. It offers no end to possible stimulations, and the biology of Earth, unlike most of the planets in the universe, is rife with diversity. It is an amazing place.

I am fairly certain that few, if any, of my incarnations have been spent on this beautiful planet. For most of my life, I simply did not feel at home here. Maybe that is because, as with incarnation on any planet and into the body of any sentient being in the universe, physical reality is so different from what we experience prior to incarnating. Regardless, this world did not feel like home for a very long time, leaving me wondering exactly what is it I am doing here? I probably won't know the answer to that question until I leave this body, but in the meantime, I have tried to gain a greater appreciation of what Earth has to offer.

Earth is rich with resources and beauty. It is a wonder in the universe, which can be deduced simply by observing the other planets in our solar system, all of which are essentially barren.

Earth alone has the greatest ability to support life, and support life it does, providing countless species and what seem to be nearly miraculous relationships between the many species. On the whole, it is a marvelous organism.

Unfortunately, we are largely unaware of Earth's unique role in the universe and its unusual bounty. We also do not realize the inherent patterns developed in nature over eons that directly affect us through our experience of life in an animal body. The animal body provides us the vehicle to more fully taste the Earth experience because by living within it, we become part of nature.

When the time came for humans to incarnate into the animal body, the initial dissimilarity of resonance was tremendous. This dissonance resulted in aberrant patterns being developed at the mental plane. Since animals are only capable of rudimentary thinking, the mental environment on earth was not well developed prior to the advent of humans. This means that early humans had a nearly blank slate upon which to create in the mental plane. Integrating the aspect of the divine into the animal body via the heart connection described earlier launched humanity as sentient beings. Because the early human experience was primarily that of survival and competition, these patterns became foremost in the psyche.

While survival and competition are common in worlds where sentient life is seeded, in the case of humans on earth the need to find pleasure became more prevalent than on other worlds. This was in large part due to the ease of life here brought by mild climate and abundant biological diversity.

The struggle that arose between survival and the search for pleasure created a dichotomy, in a sense, with two poles in the mental plane opposing one another. Over time, this struggle produced many unnatural patterns intended to achieve pleasure, but at the expense of those not earning the pleasurable outcome. Of course, this created resentments, conflict, and ultimately wars. We still see this today in our lust for resources intended to make our lives easier, even if someone else needs to suffer because of our actions to obtain those resources.

Conflict is generally considered the norm in human societies, so few question it or explore the reasoning behind it or its development. As an outgrowth of this struggle, jumbled and dysfunctional mental patterns developed. We see these dysfunctional patterns everywhere around us if we only look. They form our thinking greatly and keep us from evaluating the underlying patterns leading us to dysfunctional thinking and behaviors, with war being the ultimate undesirable result.

If we make the group effort to step back and evaluate the way we think, we would set the stage to break down unhealthy social patterns and release at a group level the emotions that keep us trapped in those patterns.

Emotional substance is attracted to mental patterns with which they resonate. One might consider emotional substance as clothing for mental patterns, allowing us to feel the thought. Release of mental-emotional patterns can be produced at a group level but only if enough people can individually release the patterns. This is the idea behind the hundredth-monkey principle.

Once enough people have moved into the new mental reality and released the emotional substance to which the earlier pattern held tightly, a balm within that group can be shared with others in society to facilitate their release from the unwanted emotion and underlying pattern. If the force of the heart essence is coupled with release of the emotion and dissolution of the pattern, the effect upon others is amplified.

Social progress is initiated by individuals. A crowd mentality is generally not a positive driver for change because too much negative emotion is normally trapped in that group mentality, even if the shared thought or ideal is an improvement over the previous thought pattern.

As a side note, it is worth mentioning that on planets less biologically diverse than earth, survival of the sentient race is paramount. There is little pleasure to be found in the natural world; therefore, pleasure is restricted primarily to interpersonal relationships. Because of this, the impetus is to build solid relationships that nurture. This is a generalization, though, because competition and conquest exist everywhere in the universe.

Competitive human interaction is merely a reflection of what occurs elsewhere in the universe. It takes great insight and perseverance for a race to overcome the dominant "survival at all cost" pattern inherited from the animal body. It is only through the heart connection that this can be accomplished effectively, for the heart connection is the guiding force that ultimately will align the dysfunctional patterns into new, healthy, patterns consistent with Divine principle.

Once these dysfunctional patterns have been released and the trapped emotional substance released, it is possible to reconstruct the mind and the emotions into a healthier configuration. This involves allowing the calming essence of the heart to lay the groundwork for the new pattern such that the mind and emotions can naturally conform to a more fluid geometry. It is helpful to have a healer or teacher assist in this process because they can serve as a channel to guide placement of the new energy form/pattern.

Some may argue that life exists only on Earth. I ask, though, "When you look up at the night sky at the trillions of stars, and likely multiple trillions of planets orbiting them, do you think that all of that was created just so one race on earth could admire it from afar?" We can't even see most of it with the naked eye!

Would God go to the effort to create all of that for no purpose? Such thinking defies logic. The idea that life exists only on Earth is ludicrous. God is obviously not so inefficient as to create trillions of star systems, then populate only one.

Creation's efficiency is easily observed by studying the laws of physics, chemistry, and biology. While the expression of physical reality is seemingly complex and certainly interrelated, in many cases the underlying physical laws can be described with fairly simple mathematical expressions (e.g. Einstein's $E = mc2$). To create a physical reality with such simple underlying principles indicates pure genius.

The better question to ask is, "Why is there such strong belief within humanity that life only exists on Earth?" From where does such a belief arise? Are there powers in the word that want to keep humanity trapped in this idea? Or is this just some homo-centric viewpoint that can be traced back to humanity's isolation for eons from the rest of the universe?

If we can accept the idea that other life exists in the universe, then it behooves us to consider what that life might entail. We know that planets can have different parameters of temperature gravitation, terrestrial and atmospheric makeup, etc.

Life on earth is built primarily from carbon, hydrogen, and oxygen atoms based on easy access to each of these elements, with an optimal temperature, along with specific levels of oxygen and hydrogen in our atmosphere and terrestrial environment. For planets where the concentrations of these fundamental elements and temperatures could differ, development of life may take an alternate path. Logically, this could lead to body types unlike ours, and certainly, a different experience of physical reality.

Look at the differences between our human cultures on different continents—and even on the same continent. Look at the difference in large mammals in Australia, Africa, and North America. Considering this, imagine how different life could be on another planet and how the culture, language, beliefs, etc. of that sentient race might be than our own.

Because of this, life on every planet is unique, so in our prior lifetimes, some of which may have been on another planet, we may have developed a pattern now attached to our body of soul knowledge that we wish to integrate with our human vehicle for a specific purpose. There needs to be an open space for this to be created. After all, you can't bake a new batch of cookies if the cookie sheet is full of previously baked cookies.

Typically, addition of such energy patterns and forms is unique to the individual and tied to their work in the world.

As you might imagine, bringing these energy forms into the human vehicle means also bringing knowledge, wisdom, and information from those previous lifetimes, even if this is not in the current conscious awareness. Having access and ability to do this, however, requires emptying a space.

At one period in my life, long before my physical illness, I underwent an internal uprising brought on by intense meditation for a period of years. In that process, it was as if my head were in the heavens and my feet were trapped in the muck of a vile swamp. The stress of the forces between these two states eventually pulled my mind apart, as if it were fractured. During this time period, one of the healers who I worked with regularly and who was clairvoyant told me, "Mark, you are in pieces!"

That is exactly how I felt, as if I were mentally tortured but at the same time experiencing the divine, and as a result my conceptions of the world were all jumbled up. It is hard to describe the experience. It was a time of mental torture punctuated with periods of bliss. I liken it to walking through a field of landmines littered with beautiful diamonds – everything in my mental purview seemed to be loose and floating about. As a result, I had considerable mental disability, even though I was healthy at a physical level, and largely at an emotional level.

This process was unnerving to say the least because it was impossible for me to be emotionally stable when my mind was fractured. With the help of my healer friend, though, I began the laborious process of putting my mind back together. This journey was time-consuming and painful at times. I struggled to find stability because while I was relatively stable on the outside, I was certainly not stable on the inside.

Perhaps this is what is referred to as a mental breakdown, but that does not accurately describe the experience. It would be more accurate to say that I was outside my mind, at least at times, experiencing the bliss, followed by a return to the mind to experience the pain. My steps to move beyond this state involved a lot of work with healing sessions and a lot of emotional release.

I hope others can take a more gradual approach to this process, but for me it developed over a relatively short period of time. It really was a torture on the mental level, and I am certain it was exacerbated by entities on the other side who were working against my development. With the help of the healer I survived to tell this story. I'm not sure I would be here today had she not taken Humpty Dumpty and helped to slowly put him back together.

Regardless of how each of us arrive at this point, whether abruptly or gradually, the mind must still be dismantled and reconstructed if it is to align smoothly with the higher consciousness. Without doing so, connection and communication between the two is hampered.

The process does not need to be as hard as I have described it, and I would not want others to shy away from pursuing release of patterns that disrupt and degrade their quality of living, but it is worth noting that working in this arena can be hazardous if you overdo it. I overdid it, largely because I was driven by spiritual ambition and my felt need to excel at everything I tackled. Perhaps I needed to do everything I did in this regard. Knowing who I was at the time, I probably would do the same exact thing again today, but that doesn't discount the fact that I was careless. Unfortunately, at the time the only person I could discuss this with who understood my dilemma was my healer friend. I can honestly say she saved my life. I say "Thank you" to her.

8

God answered, "You only make it hard because you want it to be hard."

Why are we here anyway? That perhaps is the ultimate question, one that I asked in the introduction to this treatise. Do we need to be here? Can't we just skip all this difficulty and go on to the good stuff?

Well, we had the good stuff before we came into this world, but it was boring because it was always the same, always filled with love, always fully aware, always in complete relationship with those we love, always wanting to exit that existence for a time to experience the contrast that can arise from living in an alternate reality in an individualized body such as is offered in the time-space reality.

Only through this process of leaving our Creator can we experience, through contrast, the magnificence of the Creator. In the physical experience, however, it is not possible to fully experience God's magnificence because the sensory apparatus of the human vehicle is too limited. Due to its limitations, we cannot see, hear, or touch the emotional and mental substance of which I have elaborated. If we could (and I might add there are some in the world who can see the emotional and pattern levels of human existence), our understanding of life would be more complete.

On the other hand, if we could see the subtle levels of existence we would be completely overwhelmed by the plethora of emotional and mental interactions occurring around us. We can certainly sense the emotions of another even if we cannot see them. With training and sensitivity, we can also sense the mental interactions and manipulations of others; however, we are not inherently born with these abilities.

The further we are removed from the Creator, the greater the contrast between this world and our previous spiritual life. The greater the distance from the Creator, the greater is our opportunity to learn of Its magnificence. When we gradually move toward the Creator and allow our heart essence to "pull" us forward and dissipate all that keeps us bound, we begin to experience inklings of the power behind this Source. It is a power that permeates all of life, yet is invisible due to our limited sensory apparatus. Nevertheless, its presence is felt when we look in another's eyes, or when we study an unfolding flower, or when we observe a playful puppy. It suffuses all of life, regardless of the dysfunction that may exist, leading all gently back unto itself.

Its pull is like gravity – the further it is from our conscious awareness due to the many and varied levels of dysfunction and unhealthy patterns discussed earlier, the weaker the pull. The closer we are to the Source as we release the unhealthy patterns, the greater the pull becomes, accelerating our movement toward that pull. We wished to have this distance between ourselves and the Creator so that we could enhance our experience to the fullest. We were okay before arriving here, knowing that it was not going to be easy, even if our mind and bodies cry out in direct opposition. I certainly cried out when dealing with serious health problems. I'm sure I am not an exception to the rule.

We should be grateful that it is hard, but not so hard that we cannot survive. If it wasn't hard, we would make no progress and be bored. Life has a way of relieving our boredom by bringing some crisis upon us. For that short period, we become aware of our greater self. We can use this awareness to jumpstart our movement forward. Or we can ignore it. It is our choice. Time is on our side – limitless time to incarnate over and over until we have satiated ourselves with the experience of contrast with the Divine.

Does this mean that we should engage in debauchery and error along the way? Probably not, unless you want to be spending even more time in the cycle of rebirth. Eventually, we will all reunite. In the meantime, enjoy the challenges and use them to learn and grow, for that is their purpose.

9

Man objected, "What if I don't want to?"

There really is not a choice to restore the connection to the Divine, for we are all fundamentally part of the Divine. It is our human vehicle that is the outlier. The human vehicle is like a placeholder for our experience. Without it, we could only observe, but observation is not a replacement for involvement.

Involvement comes through being present in life, despite the sensory limitations of the human vehicle. We cannot fully experience the Divine while in physical existence, and even when we catch glimpses, the experience will not be the same as when we return after our earthly life. To wish to avoid that return is a wish to fall deeper into the illusion, deeper into the separation from the Divine, and deeper into to the experience of contrast.

The earthly existence can be very alluring, for it provides no end of wonderful enticements and distractions, many of which cannot be easily experienced in other planetary realities. For this reason, a planet such as Earth is a popular destination, sort of a notch in the belt in which one's ongoing experiences can be seasoned with a flavor only available here. Of course, all planetary experiences have their own flavor but the flavor of Earth is rich and rewarding.

It is understandable that even if one were to experience the Divine to a deep extent while in an earthly existence, it might be desirable to continue on with subsequent lifetimes just to experience more that is offered here. Some in the world today are here for that reason, although typically those who have evolved to that point down the path would be here to assist others in attaining their freedom.

Freedom from reincarnation is not specifically the proper goal. Freedom to express while in the physical would be a better description of the true goal. To express the Divine at the level of physical reality is the ultimate achievement because it represents complete giving of the gifts one has brought into the world. The path to completion may be marred by difficulty and disruption, but if the final result is to fully express the Divine, success is achieved.

One's place in line does not matter; it is the final achievement that brings the reward. This conforms to the adage of Jesus that the last shall be first and the first shall be last.

How we approach that achievement, though, depends upon us. We can dither our time away, engaged in whatever fancy appeals to us, we can spend our lives in service to others, we can lie, cheat, and steal; but in the end, we will return to that connection. It is not a requirement to restore the connection to the Divine, at least not at any particular point in the reincarnation cycle. It is important however, to set about learning the lessons scripted for us prior to coming into the world.

While we cannot predict our exact path in life, generally we can estimate where our life will take us. No doubt you have had the experience of needing to do a particular thing even though you had no understanding of why you needed to do it. In fact, doing that thing may not even have made much sense. It was that way for me when I learned about the Peace Corps. I knew immediately that I must have that experience, even if I had to have my impacted wisdom teeth painfully removed in order to get clearance to leave (which I did).

I do not regret the decision to take that action. My Peace Corps experience was formative. Without it, I might not have been launched into the introspection required to reevaluate my beliefs and patterns. Presumably, I knew before entering the world that I would follow that path. For me it was the right path.

If you have been faced with such a path or decision and not followed it, you probably regret it to this day. This represents the class of fundamental paths that define our lives. Without having the opportunity to follow these paths, we would be adrift. Divine providence blesses us with the freedom to make these decisions and thus allows us to grow in accordance with our heart's inner pull. Awareness of the pull provided by our inner knowingness represents our ability to tap into our divine connection. This is important because it allows us to follow our predestined path as closely as possible and maximize our time in each lifetime.

We cannot possibly experience everything a human life has to offer, but we can optimize our experiences to enhance our growth. For me, moving to the intentional community of Stelle was another decision for which the pull was very strong – in fact stronger than the pull to join the Peace Corps. Had I not followed that path and availed myself to all the opportunities it provided, I would have missed the learning opportunities I needed.

Neither decision, whether the Peace Corps or involvement in Stelle, afforded me economic reward, social stature, or any of the trappings we normally consider signs of success. In fact, these decisions reduced my economic status. Nevertheless, the personal rewards far exceeded what I might have gained had I followed the societally expected route. In the words of Robert Frost, I followed "the road not taken" and I'm glad I did. Had I not, I would be living with the thought of "what did I miss?" by not having the courage to follow my inner yearnings.

These inner yearnings are often difficult to rationalize. Some of the most beneficial paths we can take may make little to no sense at all, especially if they cost us time and money for which there is not perceived return on investment. For me, writing this book falls into that category. I have no idea if I will ever see any benefit to myself for this effort, and yet I know that this is what I am supposed to do at this point in my life.

I encourage you to follow your heart, as I told my son when he was faced with a difficult and/or life-changing decision. The heart will not misguide you, as long as you are not confusing its message with something from another source, such as distorted or fearful thinking.

10

Man relented, "Okay, I'm ready to do this. Do you have any tips?"

There are many methods to release the old patterns trapping you. I described earlier the ones I used. Those were evaluating the role of family and society in shaping my beliefs and behaviors. I did this by evaluating the characteristics of my parents and grandparents, and even further back in my heritage, when it seemed appropriate.

Other techniques involve having a support system. Ideally, you will find someone who has already been down this path to some extent. This is not always easy to find, but if your intent is pure, the teacher will arise. This was most certainly true for me as I embarked upon this path, even though I was living in a small Midwestern community. The internet provides great access, but it also provides access to those who only want your money. Discretion is advised. Of course, learning discretion is part of the process.

Techniques that have served useful for others along this path include:

1. Listening to uplifting music that resonates with your heart. This can align the human vehicle at the pattern level with a more fundamental resonant frequency throughout. In doing so, this serves to smooth the interactions at all levels.

2. Avoiding unhealthy experiences, especially those transmitted through the media. The base and often violent nature of television and movie programming is disruptive at the emotional level causing all those "pebbles" discussed earlier to collide, rendering the emotional body into a state of dissonance. In this state, it is more difficult for the heart essence to infiltrate. In effect, the emotions block that essence, which is why we find peace and inspiration in nature. In nature, the aberrations in our emotional substance can be dissipated. Because our bodies are part of nature, it is possible for us to "trade" some of our emotional substance with the unfettered storehouse of such substance in nature. In this way, we can find a calming peace.

3. Reside in a locale that allows for a quiet and peaceful setting. This also allows the emotional body to rest.

4. Adopt a discipline, be it yoga, prayer, meditation, Tai Chi, Qi Gong, etc. All of these can balance the energetic interactions between the mental and emotional bodies, and in return serve to balance the physical body. Such disciplines work on multiple levels because not only do they balance and sooth the interactions between the bodies, but they discipline the mind.

In deep meditation, the mind is effectively set aside, referred to as "stilling the mind," which allows a clearer pathway for communication from beyond the veil of life. With this communication is carried an energy essence that is also healing to the human vehicle, although it at times can seem disruptive if its function serves to stir up dysfunctional substance or challenge undesired patterns. These disciplines are perhaps the most important for traveling this path, and they are supported by having a peaceful climate.

Deep concentration in a scientific or other field also develops discipline, as this focuses the mind, allowing inspiration a pathway to enter. This is the means by which great scientists, artists, and musicians find their inspiration to produce great works.

5. Learn to still the mind even when not formally meditating. This has been described as a constant state of mindfulness. Instead of letting the mind wander aimlessly or fixate on some idea or on the latest excitement, this technique serves to balance the mind in a regular, ongoing manner. It can lead to a gradual sense of well-being as the previous desires and distractions of the mind gradually fade.

6. Work to consciously understand your blockages and dysfunctional patterns. This is most effectively achieved through the assistance of someone accomplished in recognizing these patterns, be it a counselor, therapist, or healer. It is helpful if they understand what you are attempting to do. I was fortunate in that I had healers to work with who understood what I was telling them when I described my internal process.

I was hesitant to discuss these things with therapists I did not know well or who were not attuned to this understanding, as I felt they would dismiss or possibly misconstrue what I was telling them. For example, to explain my approach to my endocrinologist when healing myself from the pituitary tumor may have been an effort in futility.

7. Accept that you are not perfect and never will be. Don't blame yourself for what you inherited, or be ashamed of it, or deny it. I think of inherited mental and emotional issues the same way I would think of an inherited physical issue. If I were born with a cleft lip, I would seek out surgery to repair it. Why would I not seek out assistance to heal inherited emotional dysfunction or non-optimal mental patterns? Only pride or shame would prevent me from doing so.

   Having mental issues needing resolution is part of the earthly condition. Get over it. Accept it for what it is and work to resolve it. The freedom you will find in doing so far outweighs any embarrassment from admitting its existence. Striving for perfection is a dead-end. You will never achieve it, and time spent in that endeavor detracts from your real mission of realizing and giving your gifts.

8. Live life to the fullest, for in doing so the flow of energy flushes out blockages, particularly in the emotional and physical bodies. There is no substitute for an engaged life. Engaging fully in life provides purpose, which naturally aligns the three-part human vehicle with divine purpose, at least tangentially. More importantly, it builds confidence and resilience when challenges arise. It suppresses depression in those prone to that pattern, and it provides fulfillment, even if the fulfillment is not representative of the highest fulfilment one can achieve in life. Besides, it feels good. Life in each incarnation is shorter than we realize. Living to the fullest is a remedy for that.

9. Stay connected with those who share a similar path, for they can provide encouragement and support even if they cannot initiate the healing/transformation process as possible by an accomplished healer or teacher. This is

your spiritual support group. In the Filipino language I would think of this as my "spiritual barkada." These are the folks I like to hang with. They keep me on course and do not distract me from my focus or goal. Instead, they support me and in doing so teach me the importance of smooth interpersonal relations.

It is difficult to have smooth interpersonal relationships until the more challenging blockages and patterns in our nature are resolved. I know from personal experience that my relationships with others improved significantly after practicing Tai Chi daily for a number of years. In fact, relationships in our household improved for everyone. This brought me the realization that I had been much of the blockage. It was one of my greatest realizations from engaging in that practice.

10. Set time aside to relax and contemplate. In our stressful world we are uprooted at all levels, so finding that quiet place that takes us "home" is essential. For me this is found in meditation by my pond listening to the waterfall and birds as they visit.

11. Be observant. We are generally unobservant in our culture, probably because we are so distracted by all the shiny objects passing by us all the time. We can never catch all those shiny objects, so it is better to focus on what matters. This requires mental discipline, something we are not naturally prone to exhibit. Discipline teaches the mind to focus, which is necessary to give it a healthy structure. A healthy mental structure is necessary for resolving dysfunctional patterns, otherwise release of such patterns will not have a stable base upon which to rebuild. All the mental energy released in dissolving unhealthy patterns needs to go somewhere. The best destination is a healthy and well-structured mind.

12. Be careful what you eat. Certain foods and especially food additives can disrupt the emotional body because the emotional body and substance are so intricately linked to the physical body. Learn what you should avoid—and what fortifies you. Your body will tell you. I know from experience that an unhealthy and distraught body can wreak all sorts of havoc upon the emotions. It is easier to focus on steady movement forward without the disruption of a troubled body.

13. Try to find space in your relationships for healthy mental stimulation. By healthy stimulation I refer to conversation and information that can enlighten the mind as it travels down this path. Such stimulation can enforce one's commitment to stay with the process. This does not mean sharing all of one's most intimate experiences, but on occasion it is useful to share some of those experiences as a sounding board to determine if you are on the right track (and verify that you are not going crazy). This provides confirmation—or possibly correction. It can also provide perspectives that may be useful.

The perspective of another person is often times more useful for my own life than is my own perspective of my life. This is largely because an outside observer is not attached to my behaviors and patterns in the manner that I am. It is very difficult for me to stand back from my experience and evaluate it dispassionately. A trusted compatriot can provide helpful advice in this regard.

My rule of thumb is that if one person tells me I should consider a particular change or activity, I should take note. If two people tell me the same thing, I should seriously consider taking action. If three people tell me the same thing, it is a done deal and I had better get started. Writing this book is a case in point. Three people

I respect and trust for their insight in these matters told me I need to write. It was clear to me that they were correct, so here it is.

14. Allow yourself to be wrong. It is through errors that we learn of our dysfunction. I was clearly wrong in how I let others treat me by not standing up for myself and allowing damaging energies from others into my energetic space. I was defending my tightly held view of myself learned probably at age two or three. I needed to admit that my self-created view of who I was needed to change. Life forced me to do so.

In my experience, the more deeply embedded the pattern; more forceful is the event needed to dislodge the pattern. For me, that was a serious health condition. It may be entirely different for you. Most of us do not have the drive to uncover every last dysfunction in our lives and release it in a less traumatic manner than I did.

Perhaps things would be different if we lived in a society where moving down the path I have described was foremost in the social consciousness, but from what I have observed, this idea is hardly present in our society. Instead, most people are running in the other direction from this process.

Some spiritual traditions state that this is because we are afraid to reconnect with God. That is most likely the case, but at some point in the process we realize the positive benefits of reconnecting with the Divine, and the lure of the benefits of doing so begins to outweigh our intransigence toward actually doing so.

We live in a world where the majority does not want to know about the process I have described. I presume this is because it can be frightening, or maybe because the thought of walking down that arduous path is just too daunting, but the reality is that we are walking that path anyway, whether consciously or unconsciously. We can decide to hang out at the rest stop, or we can get back on the road. It is up to us. Eventually though, we will reach Oz, if you know what I mean. I can relate to that because I grew up in Kansas.

15. Let go of all the "shoulds." "Shoulds" create resistance in the emotional body, restricting free flow of the life force. These "shoulds" can become locked in the physical body, showing up as tension.

    "Shoulds" are purely a mental construct. Despite being mental, the most effective means to release them is through physical movement. In this case, movement of the body releases the tension, causing the emotional blockage to be released. If this release can occur repeatedly, the mind eventually recognizes that the "should" is more like a "maybe."

    An example of this might be the belief that I should always eat three meals a day. I was raised this way, thinking that I might suffer serious consequences if I didn't eat three meals a day. My wife inspired me to try eating only when I was hungry, and I found that not only was this a healthier approach, but in doing so, I only wanted to eat two meals a day. My belief about eating three meals a day is no longer in my mental structure. In fact, it now seems unhealthy to me to eat early in the day if I am not yet hungry. My body is telling me that it wants the reset afforded by the overnight fast.

16. Renounce all the old beliefs you were taught that do not hold up to logic. Our upbringing is replete with such thoughts and beliefs. I say "renounce" because this provides the force to dislodge them, upon which they

can be effectively released and dissolved. Such beliefs arise when we allow emotions to trump logic and reason.

This is prevalent in superstition, which arose in cultures when the mental capacities of humans were not as developed as they are today. Like the pattern of fear described earlier, all sorts of emotion-based patterns exist in societies.

It is not unusual for emotions to completely override logic. I have been surprised at times when others expressed an opinion or stance on some issue completely in contrast to known fact. Of course, I have done the same myself at times, although I'd like to think I don't do that anymore.

Emotions can blind us to reality, so breaking the belief pattern holding the emotion allows the emotional substance to dissipate. Once the belief pattern is left standing naked with no emotional charge supporting it, the pattern can be effectively released. This occurs on an individual level but also more gradually on a societal level and through this process society slowly evolves toward a more logic-centered expression.

17. Give back. In giving back, you share your essence with others. This allows your essence and goodwill to flow, allowing space for more to arise. Divine essence originates from an inexhaustible well, so there is no reason not to share it. Doing so allows flushing of discordant substance in all forms, in a sense cleansing the three-part human vehicle. It also aligns substance at all levels with the divine essence and can be experienced by an actual warm feeling at the location of the heart. Likely you have experienced this.

18. Be grateful. Gratitude is often forgotten. I know it slips by me easily when I'm facing the challenges and vicissitudes

of life. Nevertheless, it is important to be grateful because its expression opens the door to grace at a spiritual level. This goes beyond the picture I have painted up to now. Perhaps it is a topic for a later treatise. Suffice it to say that gratitude allows grace to connect from the spiritual realm to the time-space reality. In doing so, it rejuvenates.

19. Explore the unknown, for this exposes the mystery in life. Through the mystery, inspiration is found. Inspiration serves to bring light into the mental body (i.e. enlighten). Through this enlightening process, patterns can be deconstructed and ultimately dissolved. This allows new patterns to arise in line with the inspiration. It also brings forth memories long buried that bring you closer to your inner knowingness. Inspiration therefore can bring a reunion of sorts between your mind and what you inherently know. This gift of reunion is the reason inspiration often is exciting.

20. Allow those who love you to support your process, for they can be of great assistance even if they do not understand your process or if you are unable to effectively express or describe it. Their support will help stabilize the energetic changes occurring in your subtle bodies, bringing relief and centering. This also strengthens the bond you share because it exposes your vulnerability, something we are taught not to do in our competitive culture. The love of those dear to you is a great blessing and stabilizing force.

21. Try to live every day as if it is your last chance to experience life on such a miraculous planet. Doing so opens your mind and heart to the native energies of Earth, bringing to your being a harmonious resonance that balances the power of the mind, for the mind is powerful in comparison to the other subtle bodies, which is why it becomes such a problem in life when unstructured and unruly.

Allowing Earth's energies to blend with your own, which is really an unavoidable process since our bodies are part of the earth ecosystem, allows the calming nature of natural earth systems to "bleed" into our emotional and mental bodies in a way that tempers our impulses. Unfortunately, we now live in a world that is rapidly moving away from nature, thus diminishing this calming input.

22. Have plenty of tissues on hand. I guarantee you will need them from time to time because release of old patterns oftentimes brings a strong emotional response, resulting from unleashing of emotional substance that has been long trapped in an unhealthy pattern. Over time, the dammed energy "pressurizes" such that when released, the results can be explosive.

If you are working with a talented healer in this process, you may feel the energy move though you as it is released, oftentimes replaced by a healing energy that may be felt as a flush or tingling. In some cases, the physical sensation may be marked.

There is no need to be concerned about these releases. I guarantee you will feel much better afterward as this is one of the best tension-reducing techniques I have ever encountered. Tension reduction obviously will be experienced in relaxation of the physical body, and also in calmed emotions.

The more intense the release, the more exhausted you may feel afterward but it is a good exhaustion. Times when I have been able to experience such a release I consider to have been a productive day. To me this type of result measures true progress.

I'm not particularly concerned about my social status or economic position, for these are transitory and to a great extent illusion. In my experience, the inner work is far more important, and is something we can carry forward into our next cycle of reincarnation, unlike money or status. Of course, the trappings of our social conditioning would teach us otherwise. It is up to you to determine where your priorities lie.

23. Have access to lots of humor. My wife always tells me we should all laugh at least 400 times per day. I will admit I am not very good at this. It is probably the one thing on this list that I fail the most at. Nevertheless, I do enjoy a good laugh, just like everyone else.

    Laughing, similar to crying, loosens the emotional substance in a way that allows it to settle back in a more beneficial arrangement. It is a little like shaking a jar filled with coffee beans, allowing them to settle in a more compact formation. Once settled in, the emotional substance is less likely to be disrupted easily, helping us to fend off the coarser interactions in our lives.

    I don't know if I will ever reach 400 laughs a day, but I do agree it is a good goal.

24. Let your mind wander at times. Letting the mind wander allows it to rest. This can open a pathway to inspiration, especially after a period of focused concentration. In essence, it creates a blank space in the mind to allow new thoughts to anchor. It is these new thoughts that eventually displace the old worn-out beliefs.

    Old beliefs will remain anchored into the mental patterns until they are worn away by inspiring thoughts arriving at a higher vibrational frequency. Not only are those old beliefs worn out, they are worn away in the mind to be replaced by new, more functional beliefs that build strength and resilience in the mental body. Without inspiration, our minds are prone to being stuck in the groove of old patterns forever.

25. Let the universe provide. Trusting in the mystery of the creative process which drives life forward is essential if you are to allow yourself the freedom to take even the first steps forward on this path. I have found at times the mystery to be very frustrating and occasionally brought me to anger and resentment because I "Just want to know." Knowing however, cannot be forced. It must be allowed, and it is allowed by creating a space through which it can arise.

By practicing the methods I have described, an opening can arise whereby our inner knowing can become accessible to our mind, even if only intermittently. These periods of insight can be life-altering. Sometimes they are initiated through traumatic events in our lives, but I am suggesting a gentler path to achieving that inner connection, as it is much safer and more long-lasting.

A growing sense of our divine essence fills our entire vehicle with a sense of lightness that makes our previous experience wanting. How we approach this, however, is important because if forced, it can lead to undesirable results.

I am a good example of forcing my way into that space and know from experience that it is a dangerous thing to do. Instead of allowing the universe to gradually influence my movement down the path, I attempted to side-step the natural process.

Like Frodo and company, I tried to go through the mountain rather than climb around the mountain. Inside the mountain, I encountered my demons. I survived, but I strongly discourage that approach. There is a better way.

I would not want others to experience the mental anguish I experienced during the time my mind was "fractured."

26. Open to the Divine. Open your heart to the possibility of reconnection with the Creator of All. The power experienced thus is transformative and can lead to untold benefits. While in that space or experience, attempt to feel the vibration of your soul and bring that vibration forth into your entire being. This can be facilitated by setting intent to do so, then meditating or praying upon it. This practice helps align one's life with the intent of the soul, thus keeping one's life on track with the predestined script. While following that script is not mandatory, doing so maximizes the benefits of our short time on this beautiful planet.

11

Man complained, "That is a long list. Can't I just take a pill or tap my ruby slippers together?"

I am a technical, nuts-and-bolts kind of guy. I like to understand how things fundamentally work before I engage with them or adopt them. While you may not accept my meta-physical constructs, I will say that they helped me in understanding the process I have been through and continue to undergo. Perhaps these constructs will help you.

The list in the previous chapter really doesn't present anything new. Plenty of self-help and inspirational books have been written on these topics and methods for improving one's life. My goal here has been to explain the "why" for anyone like me who wants to understand the process. I find that understanding the process helps me tremendously in moving through it. Otherwise, I would feel completely lost in the mystery.

The mystery, though, is a blessing, and the more I contemplate it, the more I enjoy its presence in my life. Perhaps I've just mellowed. Or perhaps I have come to feel at home in the world so unknown to me before arriving here. I'm not sure which is the case.

Feeling my heartfelt need to share what I have experienced is the driving force to share what I have written. As I said, I don't want others to fracture their mind as I did or necessarily undergo serious disease in order to move forward. Of course, many of us will have disease or other trauma arrive in our lives. It is how we approach that challenge and learn from it that matters.

In my view, life is primarily a learning experience, but one of the major steps in the learning process is to let go of what prevents us from moving forward. I have spent far more time letting go than I have learning new things, at least as applied to this process.

Unless our old patterns are recognized, we are locked in position, unable to experience the freedom that arises from their dissolution. Without letting go of the old, we cannot welcome in the new, and without bringing in the new, our mental, emotional, and physical bodies cannot be restructured and rejuvenated to allow us to reach our next higher stage of development.

I wish I could say that at some point we reach the end of this process where we no longer need to deal with past hurts and old unhealthy patterns, but from what I can determine, that is not the case. Seems to me that it continues until the day we leave this world, although it does get easier as we move forward.

As a man in this American culture, it is difficult to allow myself to cry. I learned early on that crying was absolutely essential in this process for it, more than any other activity, releases the old patterns, allowing rejuvenation. When it comes to overcoming my fears, the fear of self-expression is high on my list. Writing this book is therefore part of my healing process because on these pages I have expressed my inner experience for the world to see. I don't know what I could do that would be more self-expressive than that.

I hope that what I have shared here is useful to you. I must say I feel a bit spiritually naked sharing what I have, but in my view, this is the most important work we can ever do in our lives because it frees us to give greater service to a world in need.

Between impeding climate change, resource depletion, water and air pollution, topsoil depletion, economic indebtedness, population growth, ecosystem destruction, etc., we need all the service warriors out there to stand up, recognize their unique role in assisting the world, and step forth to do so. I challenge you thus.

May the creative force of the Divine be with you.

AFTERWORD

For those versed in astrology, this book reflects the strong conjunction of Pluto and Sun in the twelfth house in my natal astrological chart.

The twelfth house represents the subconscious mind. The Sun represents how an individual expresses his or her basic energy and drive to evolve, whereas the Sun in the twelfth house represents the propensity to explore the subconscious mind in search of deeper spiritual understanding. Pluto represents the ability to penetrate dimensions and tap the fundamental energies of life responsible for manifestation of form, whereas Pluto in the twelfth house represents regeneration of the subconscious mind with the goal of bringing its understanding into the conscious mind. The conjunction of the Sun and Pluto supports expression of power through the ability to regenerate and change one's self through application of will power.

My day-time profession has been that of a technical writer and trainer, but my side job has been to remake and refine my human experience, primarily by letting go of old patterns and beliefs to allow space for healthier patterns and beliefs to emerge. In light of my astrological propensities, this book represents an autobiography of my inner journey.

Mark Anthony Hoffman

ABOUT THE AUTHOR

Mark Anthony Hoffman was raised on a Kansas farm, later to attend college, where he earned an engineering degree. Following college, he entered the U.S. Peace Corps where he served two years in the Philippines, learning much about the impact of culture on human development. Upon return to the U.S., he moved to the intentional community of Stelle, Illinois, that at the time, was a stopping point for a variety of spiritual teachers and healers. While raising a family and supporting them through work as a technical writer and trainer, he spent much time engaged in community building and interactions. He still lives nearby the Stelle community.

RECOMMENDED FURTHER READING

www.newmessage.org

Life In The Universe, by Marshall Vian Summers